LEGEND

the best of
BOB
MARLEY
and the WAILERS

GUITAR

ACOUSTIC TRANSCRIPTIONS
WITH NOTES AND TABLATURE

Music transcriptions by Kenn Chipkin,
Matt Scharfglass and Josh Workman.

Photography by Adrian Boot
All photos © Adrian Boot/B.M.M.I. 1995

This publication is not for sale in
the E.C. and/or Australia
or New Zealand.

ISBN 978-0-7935-3700-6

HAL•LEONARD
CORPORATION
7777 W. BLUEMOUND RD. P.O. BOX 13819 MILWAUKEE, WI 53213

LEGEND

the best of
BOB
MARLEY
and the WAILERS

Is This Love

Words and Music by Bob Marley

every day and every night. ___ We'll be to - geth -

er ___ with the roof right o - ver our heads. ___

___ We'll share the shel - ter

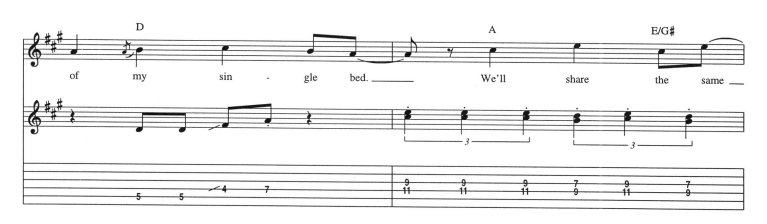

of my sin - gle bed. ___ We'll share the same ___

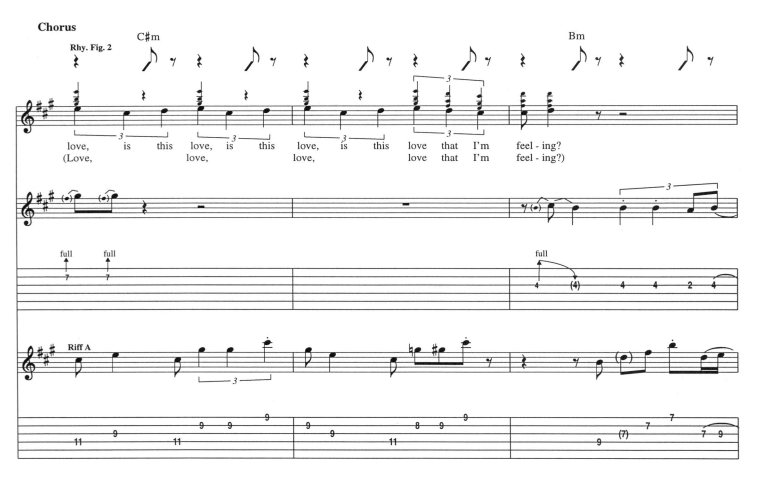

9

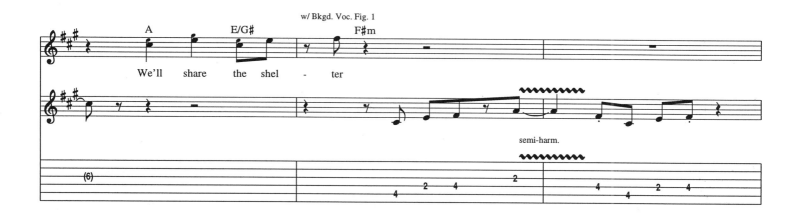

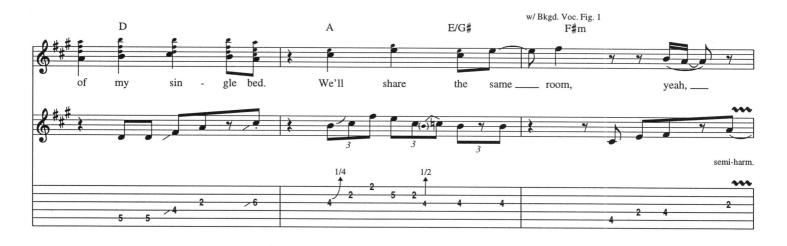

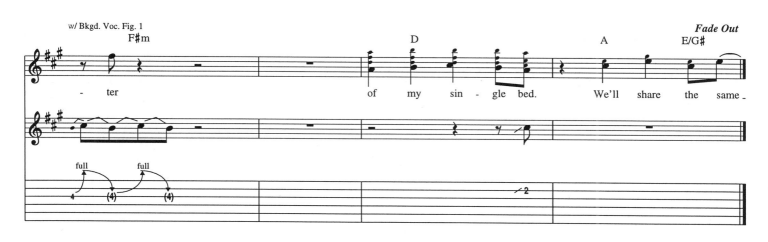

No Woman No Cry

Words and Music by Vincent Ford

Bridge

N.C. (C)   (C/B)   (Am)   (F)

Ev - 'ry-thing is gon - na be ___ al - right.   Ev - 'ry-thing's gon - na be al - right.

Gtr. 1

(C)   (C/B)   (Am)   (F)

Ev - 'ry-thing is gon - na be al - right.   Ev - 'ry-thing's gon - na be ___ al...   I say,
(be   al - right.)

(C)   (C/B)   (Am)   (F)

Ev - 'ry-thing's gon - na be al - right, ya.   Oh, ev - 'ry-thing's gon - na be al - right.

(C)   (C/B)   (Am)   (F)

Ev - 'ry-thing's gon - na be al - right, yeah.   Ev - 'ry-thing's gon - na be al - right. So,

Chorus

Gtr. 1: w/ Rhy. Fig. 1, 2 times, simile

C   C/B   Am   F   C   F   C

wom - an, no cry.   No, no wom - an ___ wom - an no ___ cry. ___
(No)

(G)   C   C/B   Am   F

___   Oh, my lit - tle sis - ter,   don't shed no tears. ___

16

Guitar Solo

Gtr. 1: w/ Rhy. Fig. 3, 3 times, simile

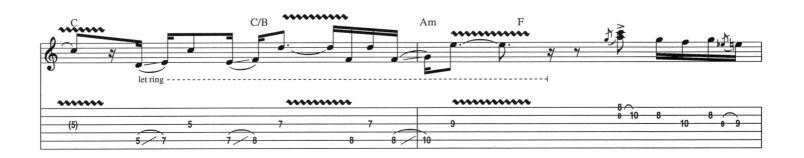

D.S. al Coda

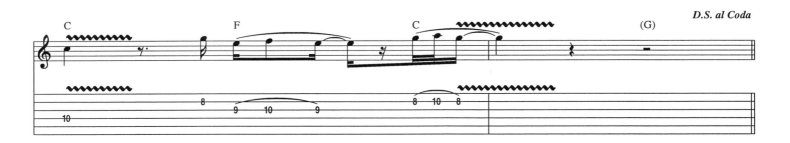

⊕ *Coda*

Outro
Gtr. 1: w/ Rhy. Fig. 1, 5 times, simile

through,   but while I'm ___ gone... _____   No ___ wom - an, ___ no ___ cry. ___

Gtr. 2

No,   wom - an,   no ___ cry. _____   Oh, my lit - tle dar - lin',   say ___

don't shed no tears. ___   No,   wom - an,   no ___ cry. _____   Eh!

Lit - tle dar - lin' don't shed no tears. _____

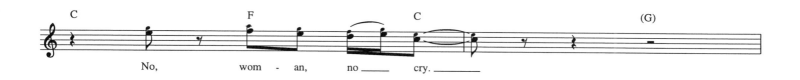

No, wom - an, no _____ cry. _____

Lit - tle sis - ter, don't shed no tears. _____

No, wom - an, no _____ cry. _____

* Gtrs. 1 & 2

let ring throughout

*Two gtrs. arr. for one.

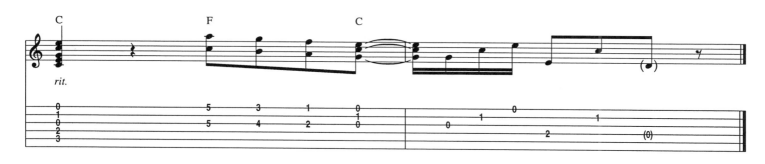

rit.

Could You Be Loved

Words and Music by Bob Marley

* Chords in parenthesis played by organ.

* Kybd. arr. for gtr.

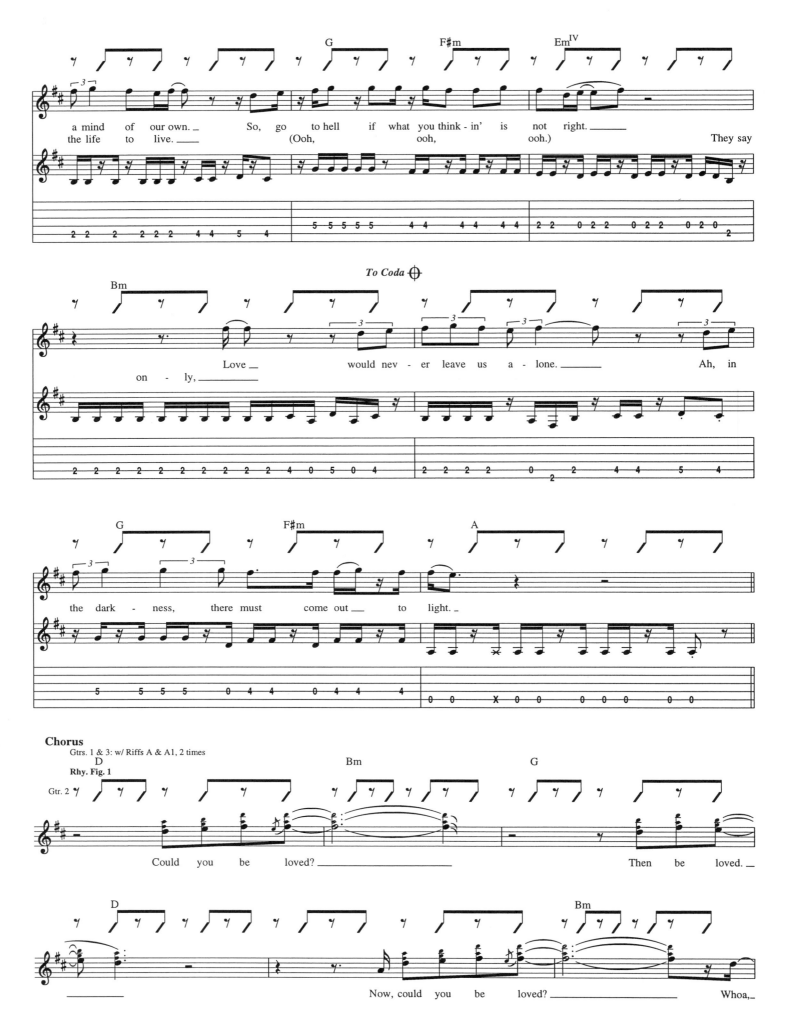

Three Little Birds

Words and Music by Bob Marley

Sing-in', don't wor-ry   a-bout a thing,   'cause

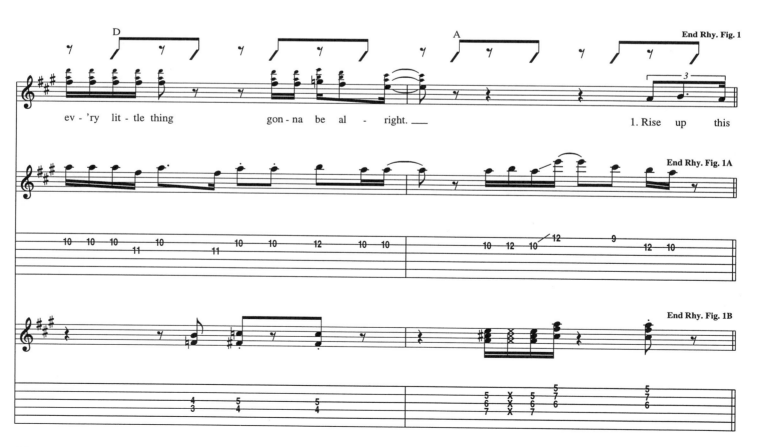

ev-'ry lit-tle thing   gon-na be al - right. ___   1. Rise up this

End Rhy. Fig. 1

End Rhy. Fig. 1A

End Rhy. Fig. 1B

Verse

Gtr. 3 tacet

morn-in',　　　　smile_with　the　ris - ing sun.　　　　Three_lit-tle birds,　__　　　　pitched by my

door-step.　　　　Sing-in'　sweet　songs,　　　　of mel-o-dies　pure and true,　　　　say-in'

Chorus
Gtr. 1, 2 & 3: w/ Rhy. Figs. 1, 1A & 1B

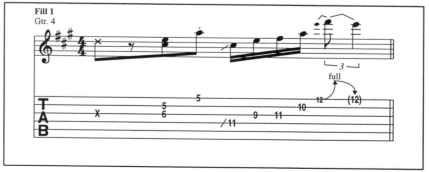

Fill 1
Gtr. 4

Buffalo Soldier

Words and Music by Bob Marley and Noel George Williams

cut in-to Ja-mai-ca,   a buf-fa-lo sol-dier.

Fight-ing on ar-riv-al,   fight-ing for sur-viv - al.

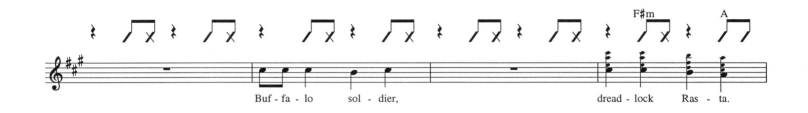

Buf-fa-lo sol-dier,   dread-lock Ras - ta.

Gtr. 2: w/ Riff C, 2 times

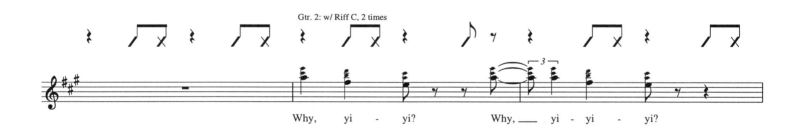

Why, yi - yi?   Why,___ yi-yi - yi?

Begin Fade

Why, yi - yi-yi - yi-yi - yi-yi - yi?   Why, yi - yi?   Why,

Fade Out

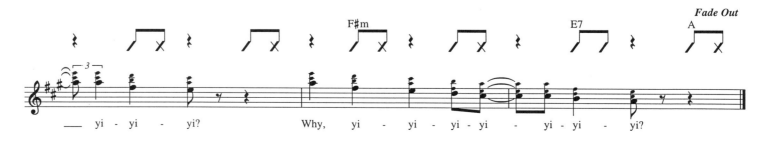

___ yi-yi - yi?   Why, yi - yi-yi-yi - yi-yi - yi?

34

Get Up Stand Up

Words and Music by Bob Marley

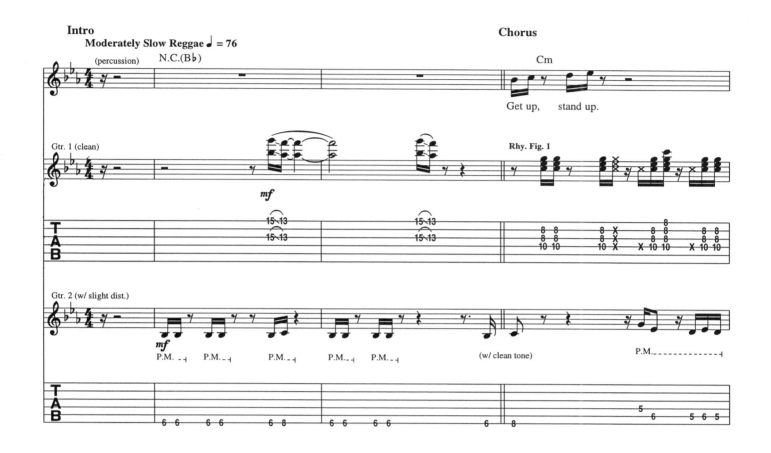

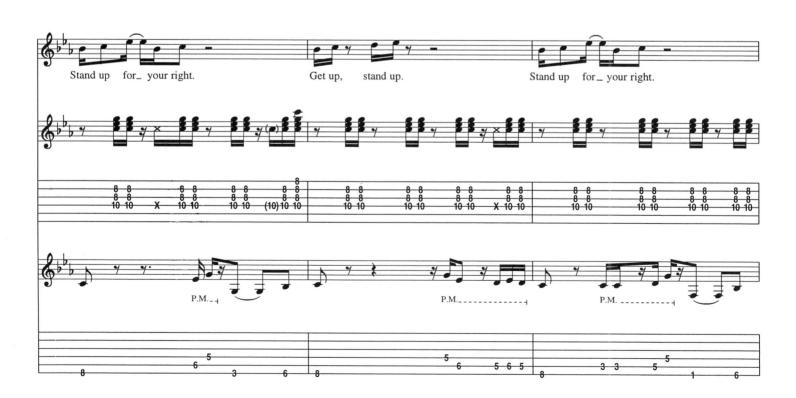

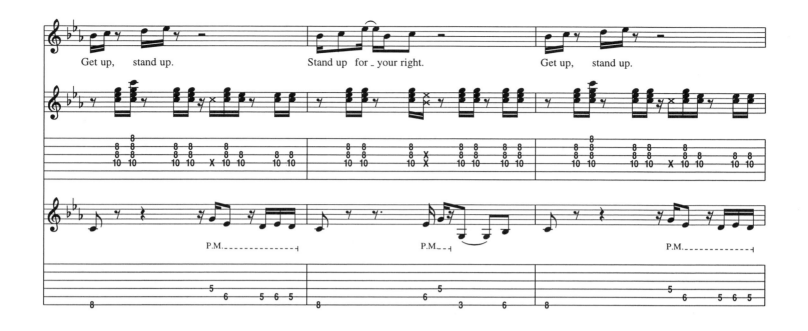

Get up,   stand up.   Stand up for _ your right.   Get up,   stand up.

Verse
Gtr. 1: w/ Rhy. Fig. 1   Gtr. 3: w/ Fill 2, 2nd time

Don't give up _ the fight.

1. Preach-er man don't tell _ me _   heav-en is un - der the earth.
2.   Most   peo - ple think   great   God will come from the sky,

End Rhy. Fig. 1   Rhy. Fig. 2

Fill 2
Gtr. 3

Don't give up __ the fight. Get up, stand up. Stand up for __ your right.

P.M.-------- P.M.-------------- P.M.--

Verse
Gtrs. 1 & 2: w/ Rhy. Figs. 1 & 2

Get up, stand up. Don't give up __ the fight. 3. You're sick and tired of your i - sm-schi-sm game,

P.M.----------- P.M.---------

dy'n and go to heav-en in a Je-sus' name,__ Lord. We know __ and we un - der-stand __

Gtr. 3

pick and fingers

full 1/4

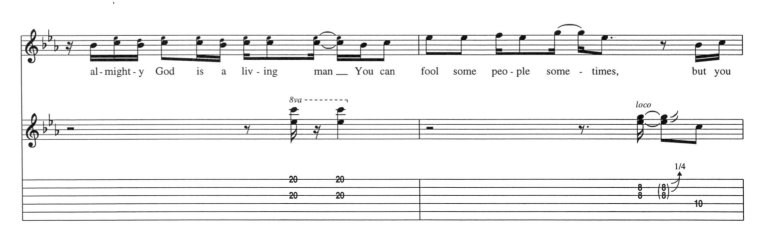

al-might-y God is a liv-ing man __ You can fool some peo-ple some-times, but you

8va ----------

loco

1/4

can't fool all ___ the peo-ple all the time. ___ So now we see ___ the light, we gon - na

Outro
Gtr. 3 tacet
w/ Lead Voc. ad Libs., til fade
Gtr. 1: w/ Rhy. Fig. 1

stand up for_ our rights. So_ you bet-ter Get up, stand up.   Stand up   for_ your right.

Gtr. 2

P.M. --------- ⌐   P.M. - ⌐

Get up, stand up.   Don't give up _ the fight.   Get up,   stand up.

P.M. ------------ ⌐   P.M. --------- ⌐   P.M.----------- ⌐

Repeat and Fade

Stand up   for_ your right.   Get up, stand up.   Don't give up _ the fight.

P.M. - ⌐   P.M. ------------- ⌐   P.M. ------------ ⌐

Stir It Up

Words and Music by Bob Marley

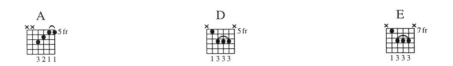

Verse

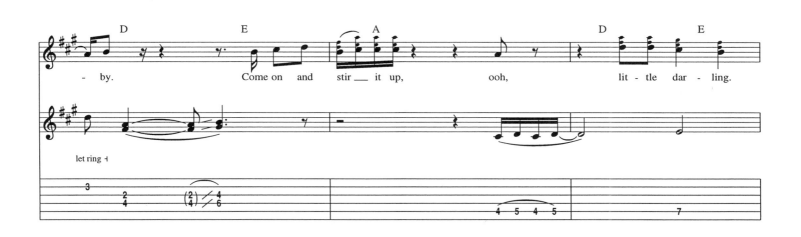

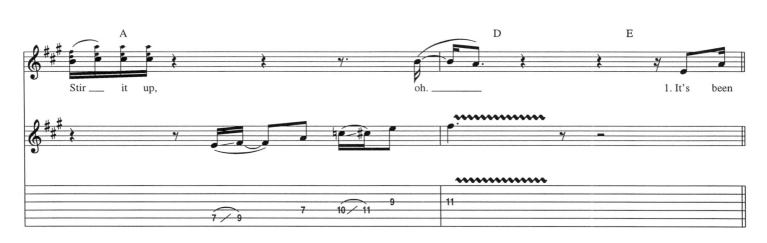

now __ you are here. __ I __ say it's so clear _____ to

see __ what-a we will do, ba - by. Just __ me and __ you. Come on and

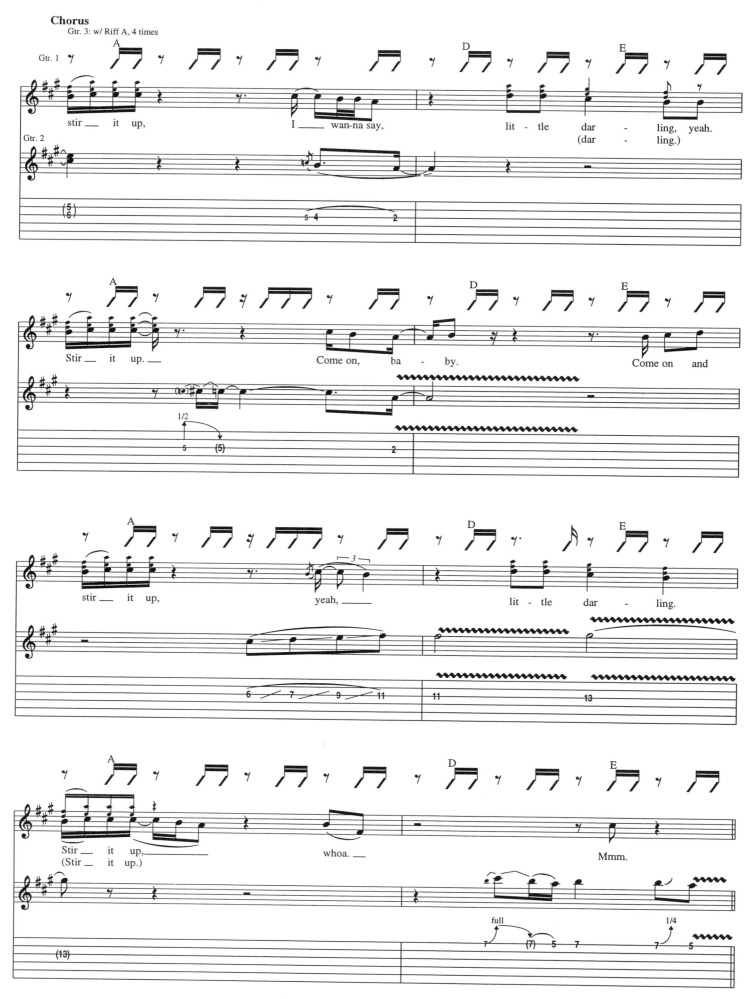

w/ Bkgd. Voc. Fig. 1, 2 times

2. I'll ___ push the wood, and I'll blaze your ___ fire. _____

Then I sat - is - fy ___ your ___ all de - sire. _____

Said I stir — it, yeah, — ev - 'ry min - ute. —

All you've — got to do, ba - by, — is — keep it in it and

Chorus

47

Verse

w/ Bkgd. Voc. Fig. 1

Chorus

Gtr. 3: w/ Riff A, 4 times

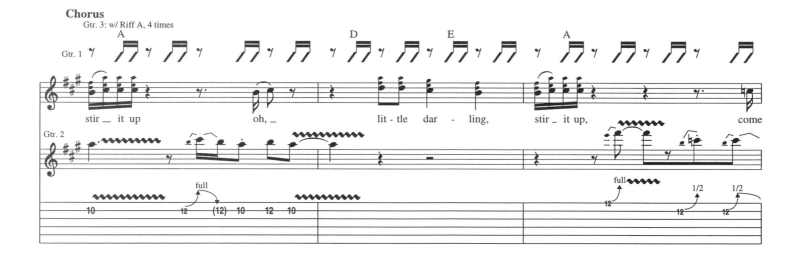

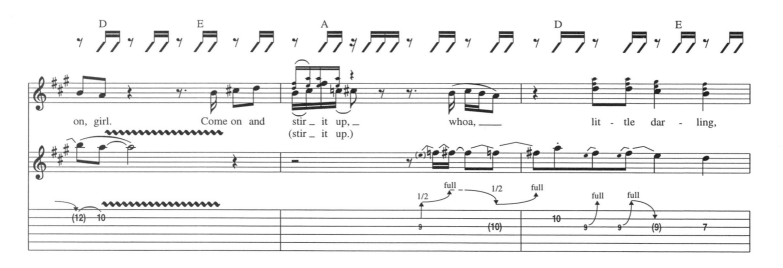

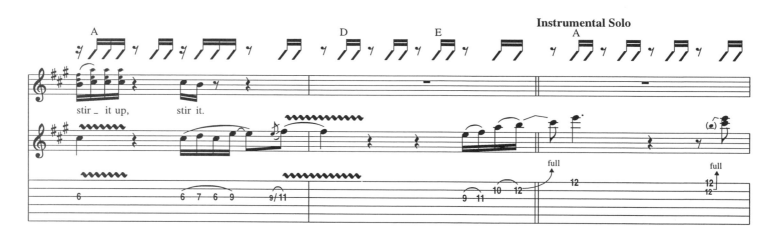

Outro Chorus

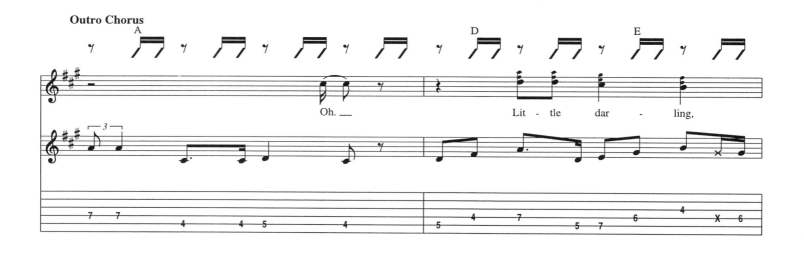

Oh. ___

Lit - tle dar - ling,

Gtr. 3, Riff B, 5 times

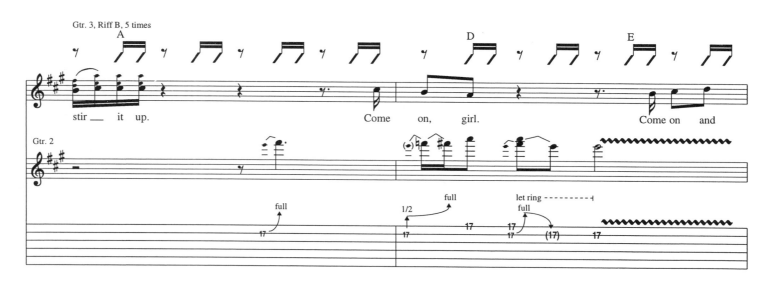

stir ___ it up.

Come on, girl.

Come on and

Gtr. 2

One Love / People Get Ready

Words and Music by Bob Marley   **Words and Music by Curtis Mayfield**

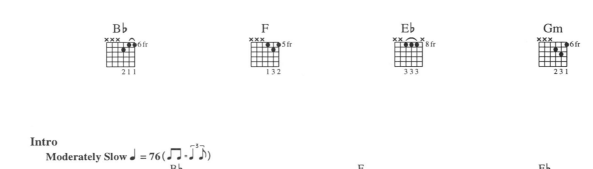

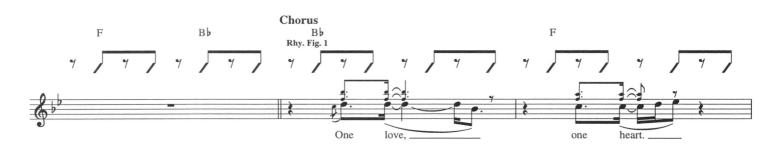

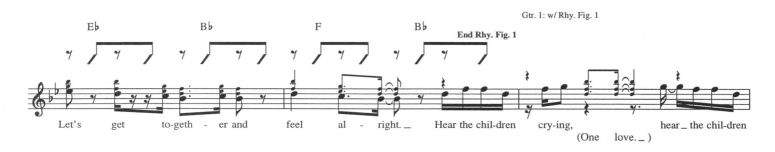

One Love
Copyright © 1968
All Rights Controlled by PolyGram International Publishing, Inc.
International Copyright Secured   All Rights Reserved
People Get Ready
© 1964 WARNER-TAMERLANE PUBLISHING CORP. (Renewed)
All Rights Reserved

54

I Shot The Sheriff

Words and Music by Bob Marley

Chorus

Additional Lyrics

    4. Reflexes had the better of me.
       And what is to be, must be.
       Ev'ryday the bucket a - go - a well.
       One day the bottom a - go drop out,
       One day the bottom a - go drop out.

Chorus I, I, I, I shot the sheriff.
       Lord, I didn't shot the deputy, no.
       Yeah, I, I, (shot the sheriff)
       But I didn't shoot no deputy, yeah.

Waiting In Vain

Words and Music by Bob Marley

Redemption Song

Words and Music by Bob Marley

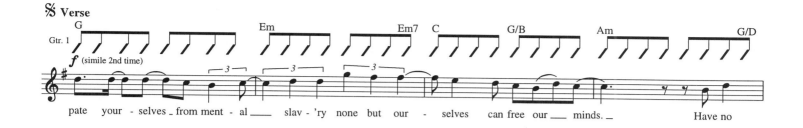

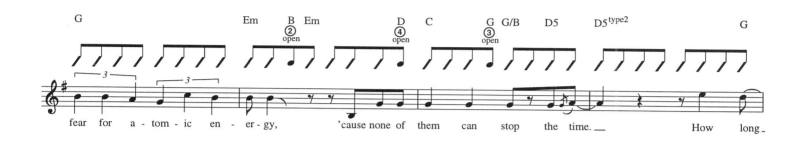

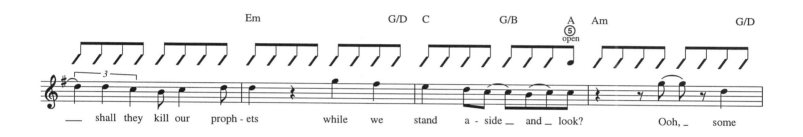

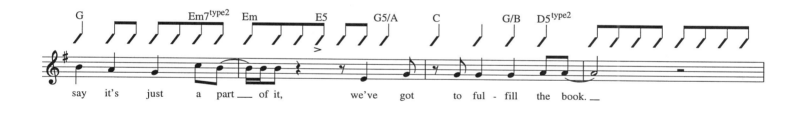

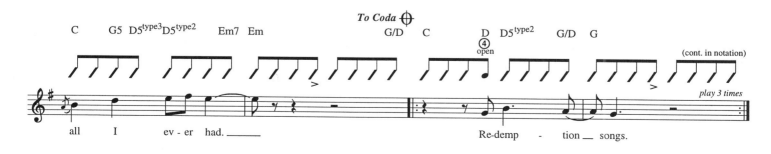

Satisfy My Soul

Words and Music by Bob Marley

Exodus

Words and Music by Bob Marley

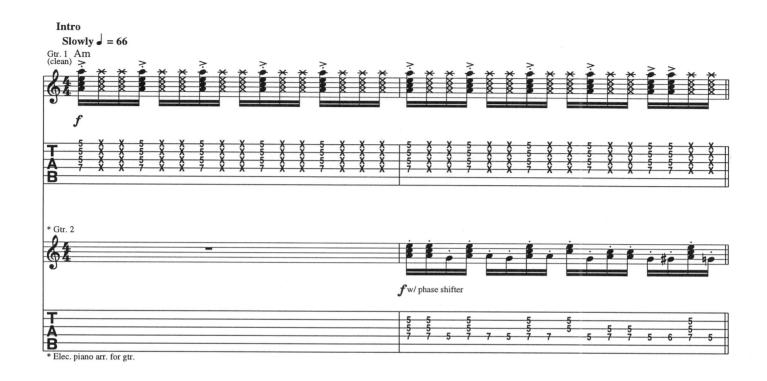

* Elec. piano arr. for gtr.

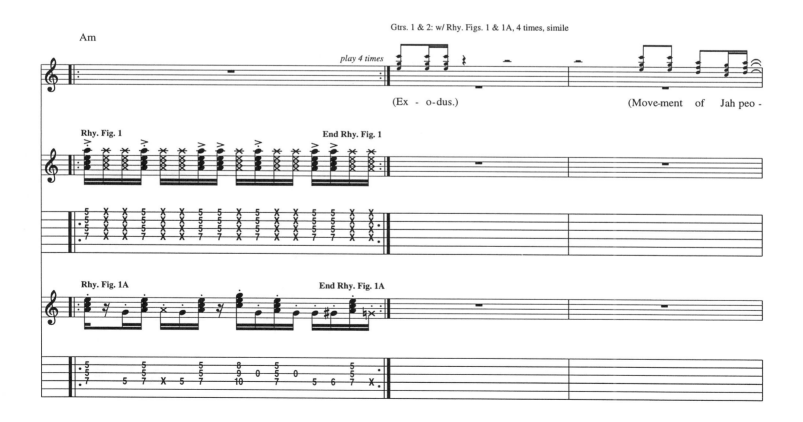

Interlude

* Gtr. 4

Gtr. 2: w/ Rhy. Fill 2

mf

w/ wah-wah

* Clavichord arr. for gtr.

Gtr. 2: w/ Rhy. Fig. 1A, 25 times, simile

Chorus

(Ex - o - dus.)   Al - right,   ooh,

Riff B   End Riff B

Gtr. 4: w/ Riff B, 2 times

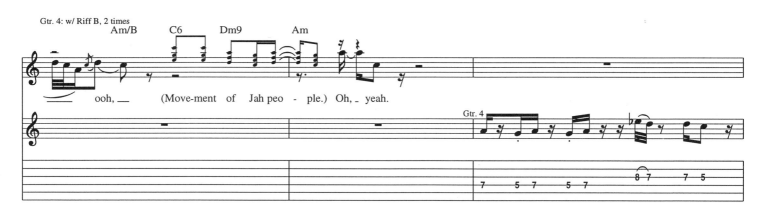

ooh, ___   (Move-ment of Jah peo - ple.) Oh, _ yeah.

Gtr. 4

*Bkgd. Voc. Fig. 2   End Bkgd. Voc. Fig. 2

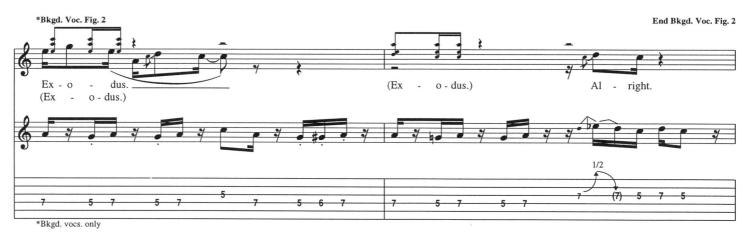

Ex - o - dus.   (Ex - o - dus.)   Al - right.
(Ex - o - dus.)

1/2

*Bkgd. vocs. only

Rhy. Fill 2
Gtr. 2

Jamming

Words and Music by Bob Marley

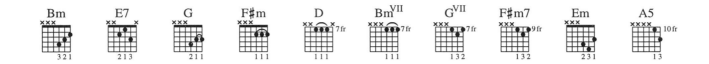

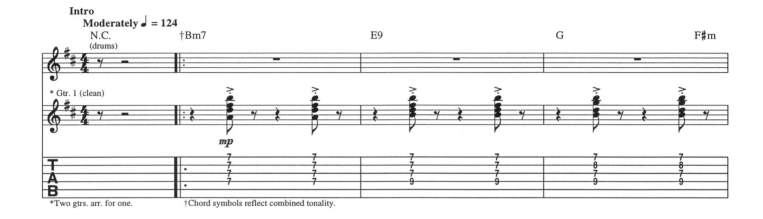

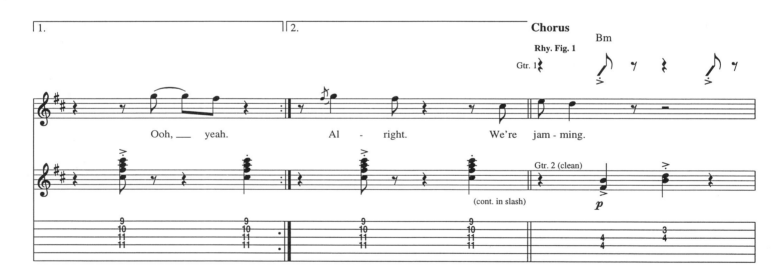

*Two gtrs. arr. for one. †Chord symbols reflect combined tonality.

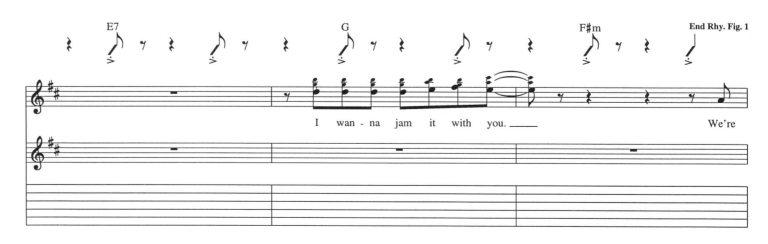

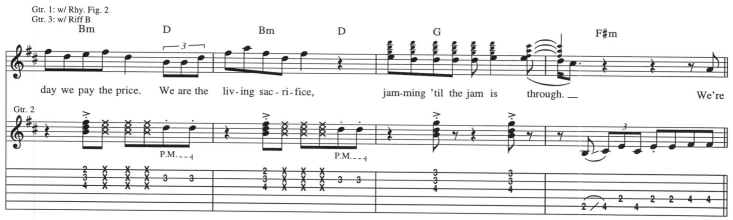

Chorus

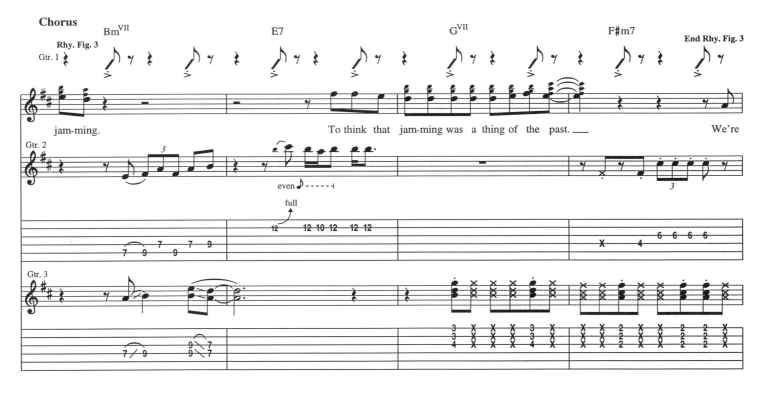

jam-ming. To think that jam-ming was a thing of the past. ___ We're

even

full

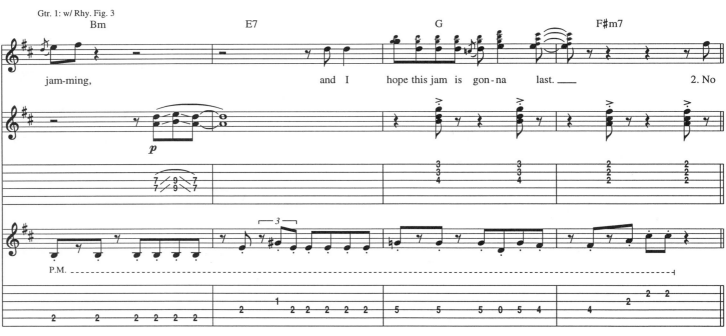

jam-ming, and I hope this jam is gon-na last. ___ 2. No

Verse

Gtr. 1: w/ Rhy. Fig. 2, 2 times, simile
Gtr. 3: w/ Riff B, 2 times

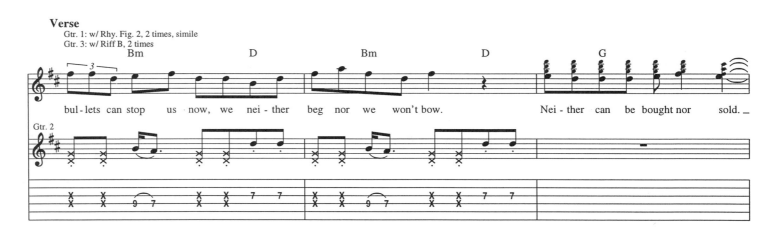

bul-lets can stop us now, we nei-ther beg nor we won't bow. Nei-ther can be bought nor sold. ___

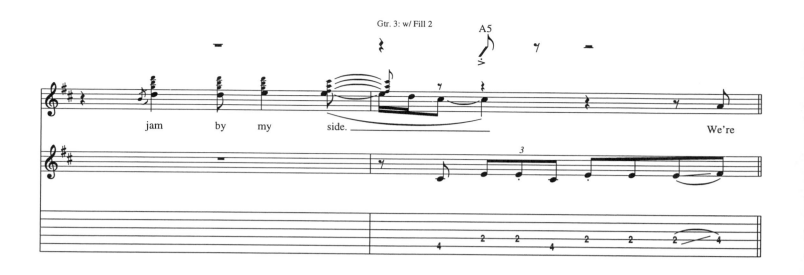

jam by my side. _____ We're

Chorus

jam - ming, (jam-ming, jam-ming, jam-ming.) I want to jam it with you. _____

yeah. _____

Gtr. 2

Gtr. 3

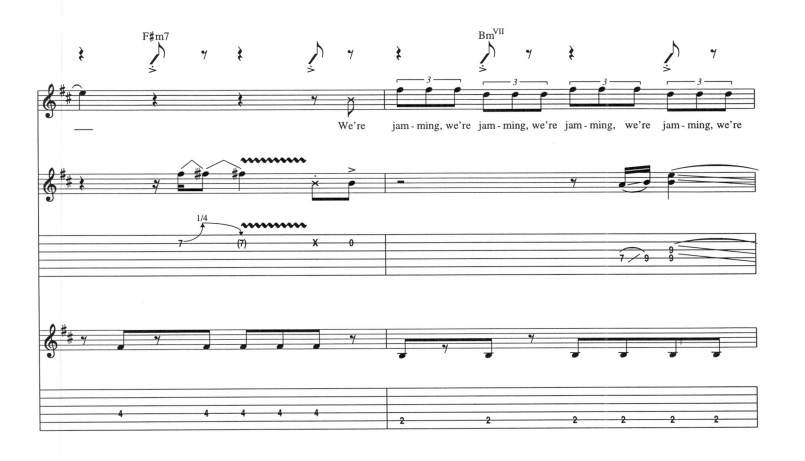

We're jam - ming, we're jam - ming, we're jam - ming, we're jam - ming, we're

jam-ming, we're jam-ming, we're jam-ming, we're jam-ming. Hope you like jam-ming, too. ___ We're

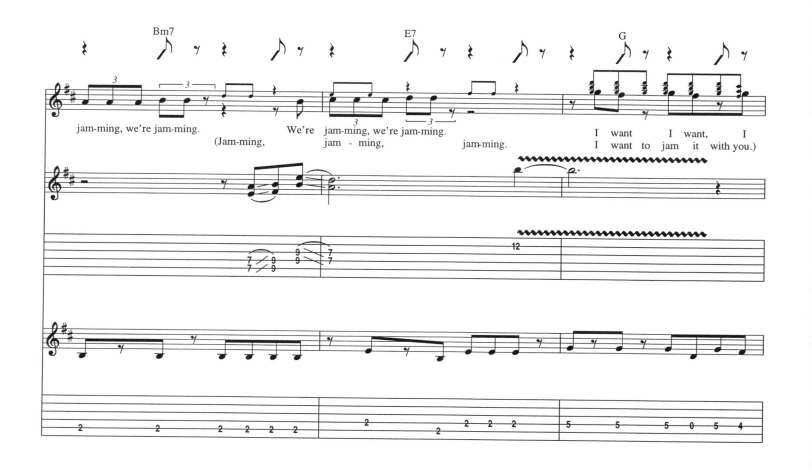

jam-ming, we're jam-ming.　　　We're jam-ming, we're jam-ming.　　　I want　I want, I
(Jam-ming,　　　jam - ming,　　　jam-ming.　　　I want to jam it with you.)

want to jam with you now.　We're jam - ming,　　　we're jam - ming.

(Hope you like jam-ming too.) Hey, and I hope you like (jam-ming) I

hope you like jam-ming, 'cause I_____ want to jam it with you.
(jam-ming) (jam-ming) (I want to jam it with you.)

I like, I hope you, ___   I hope you like - a jam-ming, too.

I want to jam it,